ABOUT THE AUTHOR

Neil Ardley has written a number of innovative nonfiction books for children, including *The Eyewitness Guide to Music.* He also worked closely with David Macaulay on *The Way Things Work.* In addition to being a well-known author in the fields of science, technology, and music, he is an accomplished musician who composes and performs both jazz and electronic music. He lives in Derbyshire, England, with his wife and daughter.

Project Editor Laura Buller
Editor Bridget Hopkinson
Art Editor Christopher Howson
Production Catherine Semark
Photography Pete Gardner

Library of Congress Cataloging-in-Publicaton Data
Ardley, Neil.
The science book of motion/Neil Ardley.—1st U.S. ed.
p.   cm.
"Gulliver books."
Summary: Simple experiments demonstrate the laws of motion.
ISBN 0-15-200622-2
1. Motion—Experiments—Juvenile literature. [1. Motion—Experiments. 2. Experiments.]   I. Title.
QC133.5A73   1992
531.1'1—dc20   92-3412

Reproduced in Hong Kong by Bright Arts
Printed in Belgium by Proost
First U.S. edition 1992
A B C D E

THE SCIENCE BOOK OF MOTION

Neil Ardley

HBJ

Gulliver Books

Harcourt Brace Jovanovich, Publishers

San Diego   New York   London

What is motion?

The world around you is on the move. Motion occurs whenever something changes place. People walk and run; animals swim, fly, leap and crawl; winds blow; rivers rush; and machines race and whir. It takes a force—a push or a pull—to get something moving, and another force to make it change direction or stop. Most animals have muscles that produce the force they need to move, while machines are powered by engines or motors.

On a roll
Objects move more easily on wheels. If you ride a skateboard, you can travel faster than your legs can carry you.

Catch a wave
Air and water are constantly moving. With a sail and a board, you can catch the wind and zoom across the waves.

Water jump
This salmon is leaping up a waterfall as it travels upstream to breed. Animals also move to find food and to escape from enemies.

On the fast track
The powerful engine in this high-speed train moves it faster than any other land vehicle.

Fast mover
A hummingbird can beat its wings as fast as 80 times a second.

Get a move on!
Motion requires energy. This walking robot is powered by a motor that uses energy from a battery. People get energy from the food they eat.

On the ball
When you play basketball, your muscles provide the force you need to run, leap, and shoot baskets.

⚠ This is a warning symbol. It appears within experiments next to steps that require caution. When you see this symbol, ask an adult for help.

Be a safe scientist
Follow all the instructions and always be careful, especially when using scissors, glass, or heavy objects. Be careful not to hurt anyone or anything when performing your experiments. When a step requires you to swing things around or shoot them into the air, do it outside, away from other people.

Lift off!

Shoot a cup into the air and see how high it flies before it stops and falls. Objects need a force to start them moving and a force to make them slow down and stop.

You will need:

Tissue paper

Empty liquid-soap bottle

Plastic cup

Water

1 Remove the top from the bottle.

2 Dip the tissue paper into the water and squeeze it into a plug shape.

3 Push the paper plug into the neck of the bottle.

The plug must fit firmly.

4 Place the cup upside down over the bottle.

8

The force of gravity pulls down on the cup, slowing it to a stop, then making the cup fall back down.

The force of the air in the bottle makes the plug move. The force of the moving plug then lifts the cup.

5 Go outside and point the bottle toward the sky. Squeeze it hard with both hands. The cup shoots into the air, then stops and falls back.

Squeezing the bottle makes the air inside push against the plug with a strong force.

Blast off!
The Space Shuttle lifts off as its engines fire. Burning fuel in the engines produces a powerful force that makes the rocket move upward.

Magnetic pinball

Make your own pinball game. To get the pinball to go through the farthest holes, you will need to find out how force makes a moving object change direction.

You will need:

Magnet

Scissors

Coloring pens

Shoe box lid

Strip of cardboard

Steel ball bearings

Tape

Ruler

1 Cut off one of the short sides of the lid. Then use the ruler to draw a line along one long side of the lid.

Put the short side back in place and cut the first hole so that it centers on the line.

2 Cut several square holes across the cutout piece of the lid.

3 Mark the holes with different colors. Then tape the cutout piece of the lid back in place.

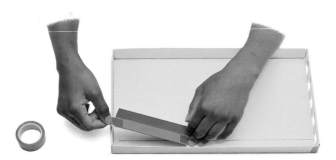

4 Fold the strip of cardboard to make a chute. Tape it to the lid over the straight line as shown.

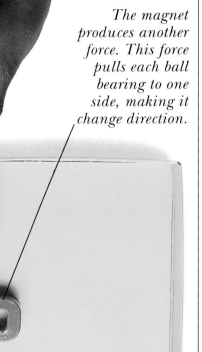

5 Put the lid on a flat surface. Roll a ball bearing down the chute. It should roll along the line and go through the first hole.

The magnet produces another force. This force pulls each ball bearing to one side, making it change direction.

The force of gravity pulls the ball bearing down the chute. No other force acts upon the ball bearing, so it moves in a straight line.

6 Put the magnet near the end of the chute. Roll more ball bearings. They swerve to one side and go through different holes.

By moving the magnet, you can make the ball bearings go through all the holes.

Pulling strings
A parachute usually drops straight down to the ground. But the force of a wind can blow it to one side. By pulling the parachute's strings, the skydiver can adjust the direction of descent.

Faster and farther

Fill a wagon with marbles and see how it moves with different loads. The same force makes the wagon move faster when it is lighter and slower when it is heavier.

You will need:

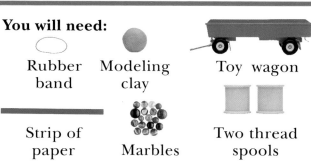

Rubber band   Modeling clay   Toy wagon

Strip of paper   Marbles   Two thread spools

1 Stick some clay to the base of each thread spool.

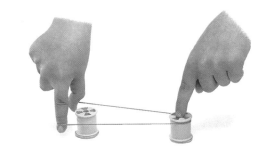

2 Stick the spools to a tabletop. Stretch the rubber band over the spools. Place the strip of paper beside them as shown below.

Mark the position of the wagon's back tire with some clay.

3 Fill the wagon with marbles. Place it against the rubber band and pull the wagon back about an inch.

The wagon does not move very fast because it is heavy.

The full wagon stops here.

4 Let go of the wagon. Mark the place where it stops by placing a lump of clay on the strip of paper.

*The half-full
wagon stops here.*

5 Take out half the marbles.
Pull the truck back to the same
position as before and let it go.
The truck moves faster and
travels farther.

*The wagon now moves very fast
because it is empty and light.*

*The rubber band always
produces the same force.*

6 Remove all the marbles and
try again. Now the wagon moves
very fast and travels a long way.

Passing the puck
In ice hockey the small, rubber puck shoots
across the ice when the players hit it with their
sticks. The puck moves fast because it is a light
object, and because the players strike it with a
lot of force.

Lazy button

Can you move a card without disturbing a button placed on it? Try this trick. It shows that objects have "inertia," which makes them hard to move. Heavy objects have more inertia than light objects.

You will need:

Large button

Cardboard square

Open bottle

1 Place the card on top of the bottle. Set the button on the card over the mouth of the bottle.

The light card has little inertia and moves easily.

2 Flick the card sharply. It flies off, but the button falls into the bottle.

The heavy button has more inertia and does not fly off.

A big shot
You need to be strong to be a good shot putter. The shot is a heavy, metal ball with a lot of inertia. It takes a lot of force to make it move away from your body.

In a spin

Try to stop a spinning egg. It's not as easy as you might think. Once an object is moving, inertia also makes it hard to stop.

1 Place the egg in the bowl. Spin the egg.

2 Gently grasp the egg with your fingertips to stop the spinning.

3 Quickly let the egg go. It starts to spin again.

When you spin the egg, the liquid inside it starts to move, too.

It's hard to make the liquid stop moving. Inertia keeps it going and starts the egg turning again.

Over the top!
This horse has refused to jump the fence. The horse stops suddenly, and the rider flies forward because his inertia keeps him moving.

Paddle power

Build a paddleboat that moves through water under its own power. Self-powered vehicles such as this paddleboat have to push backward to move forward.

You will need:

Cork

Knife

Stiff plastic

Two pencils

Scissors

Large and small rubber bands

Empty milk or juice carton

Tape

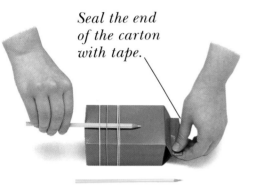

Seal the end of the carton with tape.

1 Attach the pencils to the sides of the carton with several rubber bands.

2 ⚠ Ask an adult to make four slits in the cork. Space the slits evenly.

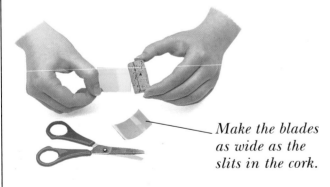

Make the blades as wide as the slits in the cork.

3 Cut two blades from the plastic. Slide the blades into opposite slits in the cork to make a paddle wheel.

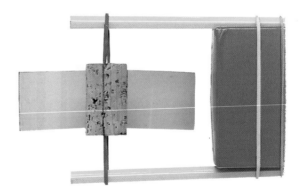

4 Slide a short rubber band into the other slits, then stretch the rubber band around the pencils.

The sharp prow helps the boat cut through the water.

5 Wind the paddle wheel, place the boat in some water, and let it go. The boat travels across the water, propelled by the paddle wheel.

The paddle wheel turns as the rubber band unwinds.

The blades push the water backward as the paddle wheel turns. This action pushes the boat forward.

Rolling down the river

A steam engine powers the large paddle wheel that pushes this great riverboat through the water. Other kinds of boats have underwater propellers. Like paddle wheels, propellers drive boats by pushing water backward.

Finger pool

Can you make a checker move without touching it? Play finger pool and find out. Flick a red checker and see how it moves another checker through "kinetic" energy.

You will need:

Four white checkers

Three black checkers

Scissors

Red felt-tipped pen

Tape

Large square of cardboard

Ruler

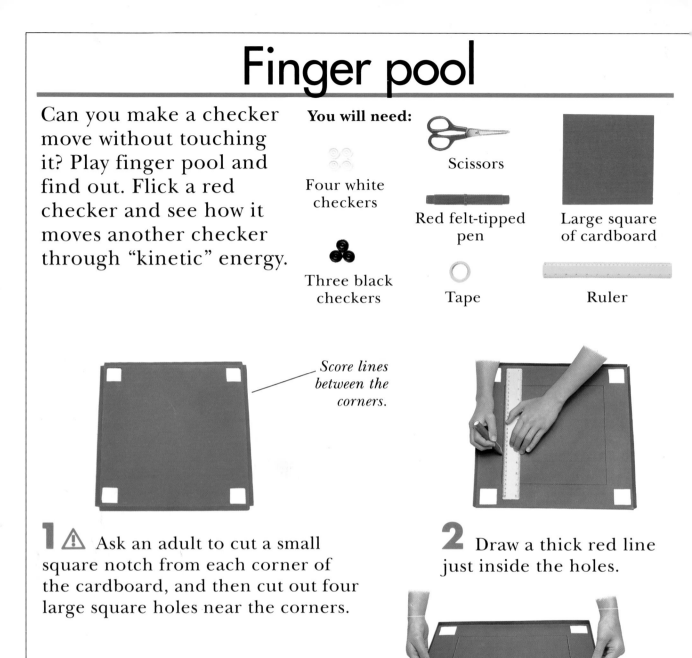

Score lines between the corners.

1 ⚠ Ask an adult to cut a small square notch from each corner of the cardboard, and then cut out four large square holes near the corners.

2 Draw a thick red line just inside the holes.

3 Color one of the white checkers red.

4 Fold the sides of the cardboard and tape the corners together. This is your pool table. Set it on a box.

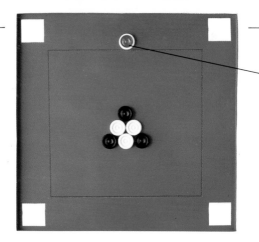

Put the red checker anywhere outside the red line.

Return the red checker anywhere outside the red line after each shot.

The red checker gets kinetic energy from your finger. It stops as it loses this energy.

5 Place the black and white checkers in a triangle in the center of the table.

When the red checker strikes a black or white checker, some of its kinetic energy is transferred.

6 Flick the red checker with your finger. Try to hit either the black or the white checkers so that they slide into the holes.

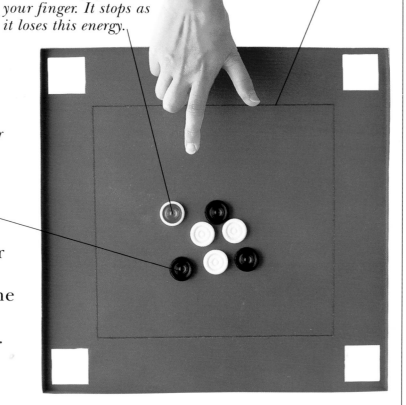

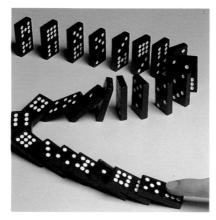

All fall down
You can push over a line of dominoes by pushing just the first one. Kinetic energy transfers from one domino to another until the whole line has toppled.

On the level

Use "friction" to help you perform an amazing balancing trick. Friction is a force that slows or stops motion. There is friction between objects where they press or rub together.

Smooth piece of wood

The weight of this half of the wood presses on your finger. It creates friction, which keeps this finger from moving under the wood.

1 Hold your hands a short distance apart. Balance the piece of wood on your two index fingers.

There is less weight on this finger, and so less friction—your finger can slide under the wood.

2 Try to make the wood topple by sliding one of your fingers back and forth. It's almost impossible! Your fingers always end up in the middle.

No slip ups
You can stand on a slope without slipping because your weight produces friction between your feet and the slope.

On the slide

Make a slide to test for friction and see how some objects move more easily than others. This is because their surfaces create different amounts of friction with the surface of the slide.

You will need:

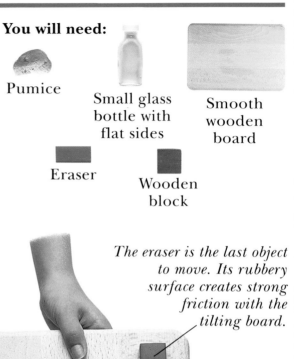

Pumice

Small glass bottle with flat sides

Smooth wooden board

Eraser

Wooden block

The glass bottle slides down first. Its smooth sides move easily over the board.

The eraser is the last object to move. Its rubbery surface creates strong friction with the tilting board.

The rough pumice creates more friction than the glass bottle and slides more slowly.

1 Place the objects in a line at one end of the board. Then very slowly tilt the board up.

The smooth wooden block slides down almost as easily as the bottle.

2 Keep tilting the board. The objects begin to move, one at a time.

Keep on rolling

Friction builds up when you add weight to an object. See how you can make movement easier by reducing friction with rollers.

You will need:

Used matchstick

Rubber band

Tape

Scissors

Stones

Rounded pencils

Shoe box

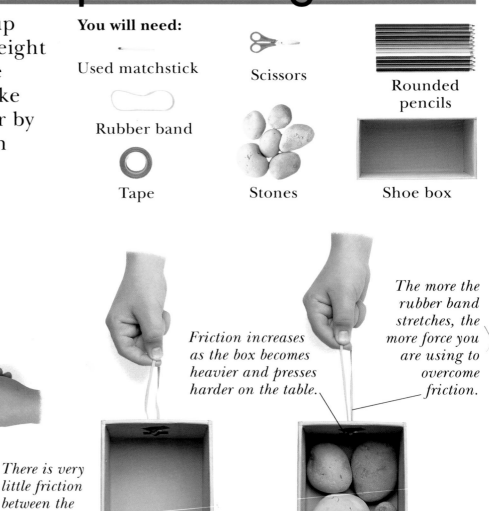

There is very little friction between the empty box and the table.

Friction increases as the box becomes heavier and presses harder on the table.

The more the rubber band stretches, the more force you are using to overcome friction.

1 ⚠ Cut a small hole in one end of the box. Push the rubber band through the hole. Loop it around the matchstick and tape it in place.

2 Place the box on a smooth tabletop. Pull the rubber band. The box moves easily.

3 Fill the box with stones and pull again. The rubber band stretches taut this time.

4 Now place a line of pencils on the table. Set the box full of stones on top.

The box rolls on the pencils. The pencils reduce the friction between the box and the table.

5 Pull the box again. This time the heavy box moves easily.

Slip-sliding away
Have you ever ridden down a giant slide? You sit on a mat that reduces the friction between your body and the slide's surface. With less friction, you can go really fast.

Swinging record

Spin a record on a string and swing it back and forth. It moves strangely. Instead of tilting, it stays flat as it spins.

You will need:

String   Piece of cardboard

Pencil

LP record

1 ⚠ Using the point of the pencil, make a small hole in the center of the cardboard.

2 Tie a knot in one end of the string. Thread the other end through the hole in the cardboard.

Use an old record, in case you damage it.

3 Pull the string through the hole in the record.

4 Hold the record by the string and swing it back and forth. It tilts in different directions as it swings.

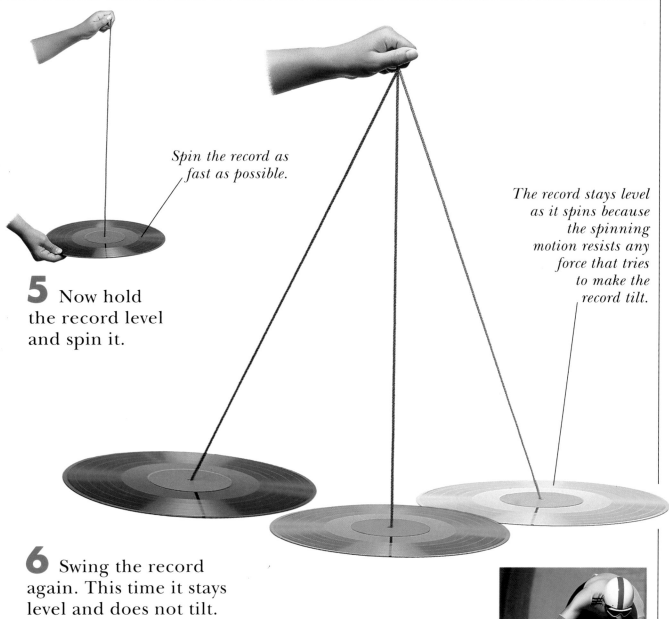

Spin the record as fast as possible.

5 Now hold the record level and spin it.

The record stays level as it spins because the spinning motion resists any force that tries to make the record tilt.

6 Swing the record again. This time it stays level and does not tilt.

Traveling on two wheels
You have to be moving on a bicycle to keep it upright. The spinning wheels resist the tilting that happens when the bicycle begins to fall over. This spinning helps the bicycle stay upright as you ride.

Wail of a time

Is sound created by motion? Find out by making a spinning disk that wails as it whirls.

You will need:

String

Compass

Scissors

Thick cardboard

Flexible drinking straw

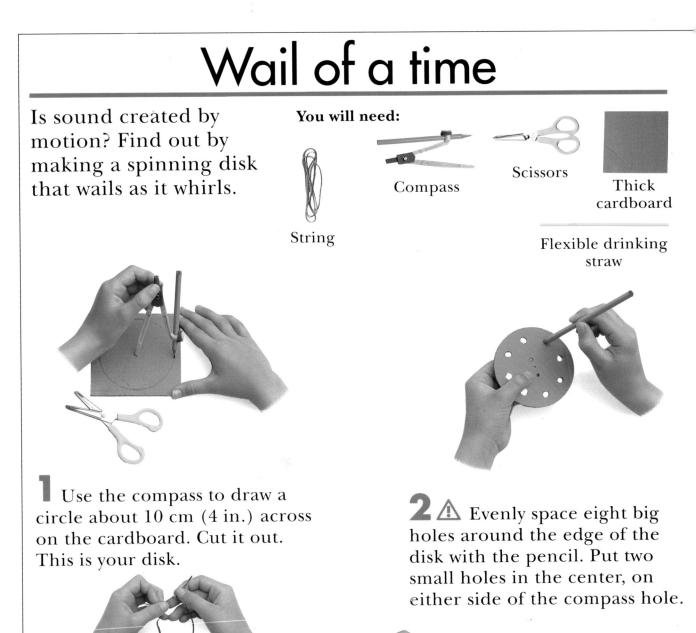

1 Use the compass to draw a circle about 10 cm (4 in.) across on the cardboard. Cut it out. This is your disk.

2 ⚠ Evenly space eight big holes around the edge of the disk with the pencil. Put two small holes in the center, on either side of the compass hole.

3 Thread an end of the string through each hole in the middle of the disk and tie the ends together.

4 Hold the string in both hands. Swing the disk around to wind up the string.

5 The disk whirls around as the string winds and unwinds. To keep the disk whirling, give a quick pull with both hands just as the string winds right up to your fingers.

With each pull on the string, you add a force that speeds up the disk again.

The spinning disk breaks up the airstream that flows through the holes. This produces sound waves.

The changing speed of the disk makes the sound go up and down like a wail.

6 Bend the straw, and blow a stream of air across the holes from one side. The disk makes a strange wailing noise!

Getting in the swing

How do you build up a really big swing? You can swing higher and faster if you add more force to your motion by pulling on the chains or pushing on the seat as you reach the top of your swing.

Loop the loop

How can you get dried peas to stay in an upside-down cup? If you spin the cup in a circle, inertia will keep the peas from falling out.

You will need:

Flexible drinking straw

Modeling clay

Two short pieces of string

Dried peas

Plastic cup

Thread spool

Tape

Scissors

1 Tape a piece of string to the cup to form a handle.

Secure the string with some tape.

2 Using the other piece of string, tie the handle of the cup to the long end of the straw.

3 Push the short end of the straw through the thread spool. Put a lump of clay over the end of the straw to hold it in place.

4 Fill the cup halfway with dried peas.

5 Hold the thread spool and swing the cup in a circle. The peas do not fall out even though the cup turns upside down!

As the cup spins around, the peas' inertia makes them move upward and outward. This keeps the peas in the cup.

Thrills, not spills
Inertia helps to keep passengers in their seats as the cars turn completely upside down on this exciting roller coaster.

Picture credits
(Picture credits abbreviation key: B=below, C=center, L=left, R=right, T=top)

Allsport: 15BR; Allsport/Jon Nicholson: 6CL; Allsport/Mike Powell: 14BL, 25BR; J. Allan Cash: 23BR; Bruce Coleman/Bob and Clara Calhoun: 7TR; Colorsport: 12BR; Lupe Cuhna: 29CL; The Image Bank/Alain Choisnet: 7TL;

The Image Bank/Paul Katz: 7CL; The Image Bank/Peter M. Miller: 6B; The Image Bank/Bernard Roussel: 11BL; Camilla Jessel: 27BL; Pictor International: 17BR, 19BL; Science Photo Library/Roger Ressmeyer, Starlight: 9BR

Picture research Clive Webster
Science consultant Jack Challoner
Additional photography Dave King and Tim Ridley

Dorling Kindersley would like to thank Jenny Vaughan for editorial assistance; Basil Snook for supplying toys; Mrs Bradbury, Mr Millington, the staff and children of Allfarthing Junior School, Wandsworth, especially Natasha Aitken, Richard Clenshaw, Ashley Giles, Francesca Hopwood Road, Matthew Jones, Kemi Owoturo, Casston Rogers-Brown, and Ben Sells.